My Friends

By Katherine Anthony

Scott Foresman
is an imprint of

Glenview, Illinois • Boston, Massachusetts • Mesa, Arizona
Shoreview, Minnesota • Upper Saddle River, New Jersey

Photographs
Every effort has been made to secure permission and provide appropriate credit for photographic material. The publisher deeply regrets any omission and pledges to correct errors called to its attention in subsequent editions.

Unless otherwise acknowledged, all photographs are the property of Pearson Education, Inc.

Photo locators denoted as follows: Top (T), Center (C), Bottom (B), Left (L), Right (R), Background (Bkgd).

Cover: ©Chuck Savage/Corbis; **Title Page:** ©Blend Images/Alamy; 3 Getty Images; 4 ©Mel Yates/Getty Images; 5 Getty Images; 6 ©Chuck Savage/Corbis; 7 ©Blend Images/Alamy; 8 ©Blend Images/Alamy

ISBN 13: 978-0-328-39735-8
ISBN 10:   0-328-39735-0

Copyright © Pearson Education, Inc. or its affiliate(s). All Rights Reserved.
Printed in the United States of America. This publication is protected by copyright and permission should be obtained from the publisher prior to any prohibited reproduction, storage in a retrieval system, or transmission in any form or by any means, electronic, mechanical, photocopying, recording, or otherwise. For information regarding permission(s), write to: Pearson School Rights and Permissions, One Lake Street, Upper Saddle River, New Jersey 07458.

Pearson and Scott Foresman are trademarks, in the U.S. and/or other countries, of Pearson Education, Inc. or its affiliate(s).

12 13 14 15 V010 17 16 15 14

I run with my friends.

I jump with my friends.

I hop with my friends.

I climb with my friends.

I ride with my friends.

I rake with my friends.